MADEIRA
A short illustrated history

MADEIRA
Story
Centre

HISTORY AND CULTURE

Flag of Madeira. *The yellow at the centre refers to the sunny and pleasant climate, and the two blue bands either side symbolise the sea surrounding the island. The cross of the Order of Christ pays homage to the two discoverers of Madeira.*

Index

©Madeira Story Centre 2007
Editor Pedro Ornelas
Design Silva!designers
Texts Madeira Story Centre, Pedro Ornelas
Translation Rosie Blandy
Printing DPS
ISBN 978-989-95535-1-4

Cover
Construction of Levada do Norte
Ribeira Brava – Câmara de Lobos
1952
Photograph: **Perestrellos Photographos Vicentes
Museum Photography Collection**

Photographs
Arquivo Regional da Madeira 35, 39b, 39c, 57b
Arquivo Grupo Blandy 49a, 58b
Associated Press/Armando França 34b
Biblioteca Nacional de Portugal 10-11, 14a, 18a, 21b
Bibliothèque nationale de France 12
Casa-Museu Frederico de Freitas 31a, 53a, 53b, 53c, 53d
David Francisco 4-5, 7b, 14b, 17b, 18c, 20, 27, 29a, 39a, 40b, 42-43, 45, 49b, 52, 58-59, 62, 66b, 67a, 68b, 69a, 71a, 71b, 72b
Colecção DRAC 46a
Instituto Geográfico do Exército 6-7
iStockPhoto 38b
Jardins do Palheiro 60-61
Madeira Story Centre 9e, 17a, 19, 25a, 41b, 47b, 63a, 63b, 64, 65, 66a, 71c
Madeira Story Centre/F. Zino 44b
Madeira Story Centre/Marcial Fernandes 8, 41a
Madeira Wine Company 22-23, 26 Photographia
Museu Vicentes 37a, 44a, 54c, 55a, 56b, 57a,
Reid's Palace Hotel 50-51
Rui Carita 21a
Silva!Designers 9a, 9b, 9c, 9d, 13a, 13b, 15a, 15b, 16, 18b, 24, 25b, 28, 29b, 30a, 30b, 31b, 32-33, 34a, 37b, 38a, 40a, 46b, 47a, 48a, 48b, 48c, 54a, 54b, 55b, 56a, 67b, 68a, 69b, 70, 72a
The Tate Gallery 36

Acknowledgements
Aida Costa, Ângela Costa
Joana Couvreur de Oliveira
Jorge Valdemar Guerra
Rui Camacho e Rui Carita

In the beginning there was a volcano

THERE WERE NO WITNESSES OF THE BEGINNING.
Around twenty million years ago an underwater eruption began on the
Atlantic seabed. In time this was followed by other eruptions until the
volcanic mass rose above the surface of the water and became a small
island which slowly began to grow. The last eruptions took place some
six thousand years ago and nowadays the volcanoes are dormant.
Therefore, the island of Madeira is the top of a mountain which rises
5000 metres above the ocean floor. Only two fifths of this mountain

The peaks in the centre of the island are severely eroded vestiges of some of the island's largest volcanoes

are above the water. The island covers an area of 728 km² and, between its extremities, it is 58 km long and 23 km wide.

Its highest point is Pico Ruivo which stands at 1,861 metres. There are around 250 thousand inhabitants. The island is located 978 km southwest of Lisbon and 796 km off the Moroccan coast, approximately on the same latitude as Casablanca. The archipelago also includes the small island of Porto Santo and the Desertas and Selvagens Islands, the latter two groups being uninhabited. The climate in Madeira is strongly influenced by the Gulf Stream which contributes to the mild winters on account of the predominant winds – the northeast trade winds – and by the shape of the terrain which is quite steep and almost perpendicular to these winds. This means that the north of the island, which is exposed to the trade winds, is colder and wetter than the south side, which is almost completely sheltered.

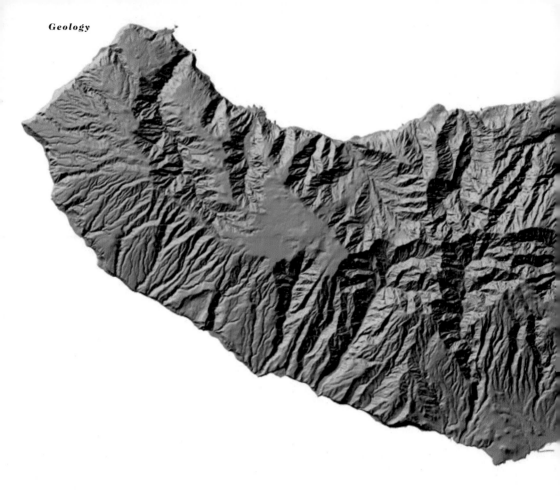

Volcanic activity on the island

VOLCANIC activity in Madeira alternated between explosive phases in which the pyroclasts - a variety of not very dense materials – ashes, scoriae, bombs – were violently expelled and effusive phases in which lava was emitted, giving rise, when cool, to basalt flows. When the lava rises, it passes through the various formations, resulting in networks of (vertical) dykes and (horizontal) seams. Erosion caused by flowing water has destroyed the majority of the volcanic edifices, excavating deep valleys whose width is determined by the softness of the rock.

There are three significant large groups: the central volcanic massif with the island's highest peaks such as Pico Ruivo and Pico do Areeiro where the biggest volcanoes existed; the western group separated from the central group by the large valleys of Ribeira Brava and São Vicente and dominated by the Paúl da Serra plateau; and the eastern area which ends at Ponta de São Lourenço. The lava columns are clearly visible in the area of the high peaks. This results in a spectacular, enormous grid which can be seen, for example, from the path from Pico do Areeiro to Pico Ruivo. Arco da Calheta and Arco de São Jorge, originally understood to be old volcanic craters that had been partially demolished by sea erosion, are no more than large landslides resulting from the action of gravity on the slopes. The rest was demolished by sea erosion.

*Digital model of the **surface of Madeira and Porto Santo**. The following features stand out: in the middle, the central massif which is very steep and eroded; the Paúl da Serra plateau to the west; Ribeira da Janela to the northeast; Ribeira Brava to the southeast and Ribeira dos Socorridos in the middle to the south. All these ravines are wider at the source where there is softer volcanic material and narrow towards the mouth where they encountered more resistent basalt. In the Funchal area the small volcanic cones to the west of the city can be seen.*

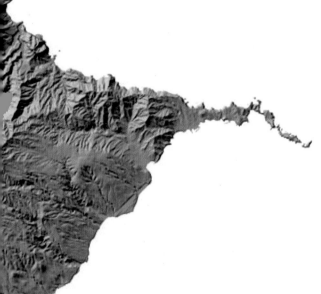

The volcanoes of Funchal

THE LAST phase of volcanic activity took place all over the island. Some volcanic cones from this era such as the hills to the west of Funchal are clearly visible – Pico de São Martinho, Pico da Cruz and Pico dos Barcelos as well as the Mole islet in Porto Moniz and the Santo da Serra lagoon. In Caniço and Ponta de São Lourenço there are volcanic cones which have been partially destroyed by the sea, revealing by the sea, revealing the rise of the lava between the scoriae.

Sea erosion

Fajã da Penha d'Águia

THE HIGH sea cliffs found almost all the way along the coast (80%) result from the sea erosion to which the island is permanently subject, causing the cliffs to collapse sometimes creating flat stretches of land at their base (fajãs). The photograph shows a recent "fajã" created by the collapse of Penha d'Águia on the northeast of the island in 1992.

The same but different

VOLCANIC rocks are all made from magma expelled by volcanoes, which, on cooling and solidifying, result in different types of rock. One of the most basic differences arises from the rocks originating from effusive or explosive eruptions. In the first instance flows or streams are formed and, in the second, pyroclasts which are classified by the size of the material expelled – from the finest – ashes – via lapilli, to the most solid – bombs. Pyroclasts are severely affected by erosion while the more resistant flows or seams tend to form crests which correspond to the peaks.

Columnar jointed basalt   *Basalt*   *Lapilli tuffs (soft building stone)*   *Volcanic bomb*

Why is there white sand on Porto Santo?

Volcanic activity on this island ceased long before that on Madeira. The beach is the result of calcareous materials originating from marine organisms that existed at a time when the climate was much hotter and which, over time, were deposited on the south coast

Madeira is put on the map

FROM THE XIIIth century onwards the West African coast was explored by the people of the Mediterranean and the XIVth century saw the production of the first Italian and Catalan charts and portolans on which the archipelagos of Madeira and the Canaries were marked. It is therefore very probable that the Portuguese knew that Madeira existed long before but its official discovery and the beginning of its colonisation only took place in 1420. It was the first step in an epic which was to culminate at the beginning of the next century with the discovery of the maritime route to India and the construction of the Portuguese maritime commercial empire.

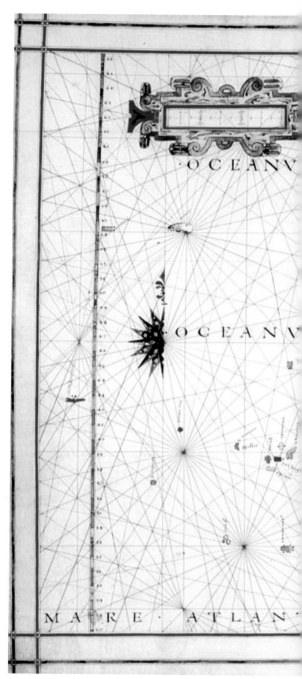

Atlas dating from circa 1575 attributed to Fernão Dourado, a Portuguese cartographer of India. Special mention goes to the system of wind roses and rhumb lines typical of portolans instead of the grid with longitude and latitude coordinates used in modern maps

From myth to reality

Ancient history refers to the existence
of islands in the Atlantic in the form of
legends and mythological reports of which
the best known is that of Atlantis, the
large island destroyed by a cataclysm
which is mentioned by Plato. Other
naturalist Greek and Roman philosophers
such as Diodorus of Sicily, Strabo and
Plutarch also mention the existence
of islands in the Atlantic Ocean. In this
Greco-Roman tradition there are
references to mythical islands such as
the Fortunate Islands, St. Brendan's Island

or Brazil Island. It is possible that these
myths were founded on factual knowledge
which may have been related to Madeira
or the Canaries. The Middle Ages saw the
appearance of the first reports of journeys
to these islands in the Atlantic including
one expedition financed by the Portuguese
king, Afonso IV, in 1341, led by Italian
captains with a crew of Castilians,
Aragonese-Catalans and Portuguese.
The islands of the Madeira archipelago
then began to feature on maps as did
those of the Canaries

Page of the 1375 Catalan Atlas attributed to Abraham Cresques, a Jewish cartographer from Majorca.
Madeira ("Insula de Legname") can be seen at the top of the image along with the Desertas and Selvagens Islands

Rediscovering...

IN *Crónica da Guiné* (1448) Gomes Eanes de Azuzura recounts that two squires who took part in the conquest of Ceuta, João Gonçalves Zarco and Tristão Vaz Teixeira, were sent to explore the African coast by Prince Henry the Navigator in 1419. Diverted by a storm they happened on the Island of Porto Santo. On their return to Portugal they told the prince that the island was suitable for colonisation; he instructed them to return and take possession of the island in his name. This they did the following year along with a third navigator, the nobleman of Italian origin, Bartolomeu Perestrelo.
A year later they moved to the neighbouring island of Madeira which they found to be very fertile and abundant in water. They informed the prince who immediately dispatched "other people" to occupy the island.

Caravels, easy to handle and capable of sailing close to the wind, were most commonly used during the first period of the Discoveries. Once the sea routes became known, ships with round sails that were faster with a following wind became commonplace. Drawings by Rear-Admiral João Brás de Oliveira, 1894

... the discovery

GIVEN THAT the islands of the archipelago had already featured on maps since the XIVth century it is unlikely that the Portuguese had no knowledge of them. Furthermore, to the south the Canaries were already known to the Portuguese and the Spanish and their possession was the subject of a dispute between the two kingdoms. It is also probable that Portuguese ships had seen Madeira when returning to Portugal. It is presumed that by stating their prior ignorance of the islands the chroniclers sought to reinforce the legitimacy of Portuguese occupation, pre-empting the Spanish and avoiding conflict. It is also possible that the Portuguese knew of Madeira's existence but not its precise location.

The first stage of the Discoveries

PRECEDED by the conquest of Ceuta, the colonisation of Madeira from 1420 to 1425 marked the first stage of the Discoveries. From now on Portuguese ships ventured further south in search of African gold, slaves and the passage from the Atlantic to the Indian Ocean, which they finally discovered some decades later – a project which gave rise to the Portuguese commercial empire. The thinking at the time saw maritime expansion as a continuation of the religious war against the Muslims – in fact the Order of Christ succeeded the Order of the Temple in Portugal and was one of the military religious orders that contributed to the expulsion of the Muslims from Portuguese territory.

*Portrait of **Prince Henry the Navigator** in* Crónica do Descobrimento e Conquista da Guiné *by the Viscount of Santarém (1841)*

Prince Henry the Navigator

Prince Henry the Navigator (1394-1460) was the key figure in Portuguese overseas expansion during the XVth century. Son of King João I, he directed and financed the exploratory expeditions in the Atlantic beginning with the conquest of Ceuta in 1415. Appointed governor of this stronghold and of the Algarve as well as Grand Master of the Order of Christ by King Duarte, his brother, he settled with his following of navigators, astronomers and merchants in Lagos in the Algarve; from here he directed Portugal's expansionist strategy. In 1433 he became feudal lord of Madeira with the right to exercise justice and charge taxes, bringing the island under the jurisdiction of the Order of Christ.

*Madeira's longstanding association to the **Order of Christ** is still visible today in the traditional banners which decorate the "arraiais" (street festivals) as well in the autonomous region's flag*

"Weighing the sun" with an astrolabe and observation with a cross-staff (another instrument used for measuring the height of the stars) engraving by Hans Staden, 1557

New technologies

THE VOYAGES undertaken by Prince Henry the Navigator in the XVth century used a series of technological innovations, bringing together Arab, Roman and North European know-how which permitted navigation out of sight of land. The characteristics of the coast and reference points were compiled into maps called portolans that showed the courses to be followed from one point to another by means of wind roses aided by a compass. The stars were also used to navigate. The astrolabe and the quadrant, which permitted the latitude to be calculated

from the angle of the sun or the North Star with the horizon, were used from 1450 onwards. Caravels modelled on Arab vessels were developed by the Portuguese as from the beginning of the XVth century. They were light ships of about 50 tonnes with a crew of around 20 men and lateen sails which made them easier to manoeuvre and enabled them to sail close to the wind. Once the wind system in the Atlantic had been understood larger ships with square sails which were faster with a following wind were used.

Quadrant

The quadrant was a simple instrument which permitted sailors to measure the latitude of their location. By pointing the sights at the North Star or at the sun at midday a scale on the quadrant showed the angle the star made with the horizon from which the latitude could be calculated.

Compass

Probably of Chinese origin, this essential instrument was introduced into the Mediterranean by the Arabs where it became commonplace in the XIIIth century.

Portolan

Portolans contained maps of the coast, written instructions for navigation and the location of ports as well as courses to be steered, using a characteristic system of wind roses.

Astrolabe

A successor to the quadrant, the astrolabe was also used to calculate the latitude. This is a model of a cast iron astrolabe dating from around 1588; the interior of the disc has been excised to reduce resistance to the wind.

Columbus in Madeira

Columbus' house. *João Esmeraldo's house was demolished in the XIXth century. One of the windows is on display at Quinta da Palmeira (a neighbouring property)*

The three captaincies

IN 1478, long before the journey to America which made him famous, Christopher Columbus came to Funchal seeking to buy sugar for Genovese merchants. While there he married Filipa Moniz, daughter of Bartolomeu Perestrelo. According to Bartolomé de las Casas, Columbus and his wife lived for some time in Porto Santo where their son was born in 1482. Columbus was but one of many navigators and merchants from the contemporary European commercial powers – Florence, Genova, Venice and Flanders – who transported sugar from Madeira to the European ports. Some of them established themselves in Madeira including Jean d'Esmenault from Flanders who settled here in 1480 and got married. He changed his surname to Esmeraldo to make it more Portuguese and became a big landowner in a place which became known as Lombada do Esmeraldo in Ponta do Sol; he was made a nobleman of the royal household. The story goes that Columbus stayed in a large house which Esmeraldo owned in the street which bears his name in the Sé parish.

Statue of João Gonçalves Zarco in Funchal by Francisco Franco, 1928

IMMEDIATELY after the onset of colonisation Madeira was divided into two captaincies by a diagonal line running from the northwest to the southeast between Porto Moniz and Caniço. João Gonçalves Zarco was given the captaincy of Funchal on the western side and Tristão Vaz Teixeira that of Machico on the eastern side. The Island of Porto Santo was considered a third captaincy which was given to Bartolomeu Perestrelo. The captaincies were passed down within the family and the feudal lords of the provinces had the power to administer justice (up to a certain point such as the death sentence) as well as to endow and lease land for farming. They also held the monopoly over mills, ovens and presses. It was a pioneering system of colonial administration.

The last feudal lord of Madeira

ON HIS DEATH, Prince Henry the Navigator's titles of Duke of Viseu, Grand Master of the Order of Christ and feudal lord of Madeira passed to his nephew and adopted son, Fernando and his descendants. In 1484 the last duke, Diogo, was accused of conspiracy and stabbed to death with a dagger by King João II himself. Diogo's younger brother, Manuel (1469-1521), Duke of Beja, became the new Grand Master of the Order of Christ and feudal lord of Madeira. On the death of King João II without issue Manuel ascended to the throne in 1495 and continued the expansionist policies. In 1497 Manuel incorporated Madeira into the crown. Funchal cathedral was built at his instigation on land donated by him. During Manuel's reign the Portuguese navigators reached Brazil and the east coast of Africa; they took possession of Goa in India and other strongholds in the Indian Ocean, establishing a commercial empire. Manuel's era also became associated with an original, late Gothic architectural style known as "Manueline".

Engraving from "3.º Livro das Ordenações Manuelinas" showing **King Manuel I** *presiding over a trial*

Manueline doors *in Rua dos Barreiros in Santa Maria and the old Funchal customs house on the corner of Avenida do Mar and Rua António José de Almeida*

The empire's first Cathedral

The construction of the **Funchal Cathedral** began in 1493 on land donated by the future King Manuel I; it was consecrated in 1517. Between 1514 and 1551 it was the seat of a huge diocese which came to include all the fortresses and territories conquered by the Portuguese from Brazil to Africa and Asia

Pirate attack!

THERE are records of pirate attacks on Madeira dating from the XVIth century onwards – first the French, then the English, Dutch and Algerians partly reflecting international political events. One of the most famous attacks took place in 1566 when a French expedition supposedly exploring the African coast led by Captain Peyrot de Monluc (also known as Bertrand de Montluc, son of the famous Blaise de Monluc, Marshal of France) put Funchal under sword and fire, looting everything they could. Monluc was mortally wounded during the attack on the São Lourenço Fortress after 16 days of bloody violence. Porto Santo was subjected to another famous attack. In 1617 a fleet of Algerian pirates attacked the island, kidnapping the whole population – around 900 people – who remained captive in Algeria for many years awaiting rescue. Many never returned. At the time this kind of behaviour by Maghreb pirates was common; they kidnapped defenceless communities especially on the north coast of the Mediterranean and sold them as slaves or took them hostage. In Portugal there was even an institution connected to the Church dedicated to paying ransoms; it had Arabic speaking priests who would go to Algeria to negotiate the liberation of the captives.

Madeira defends itself

FOLLOWING the attack by the French pirates in 1566 the city of Funchal was fortified with a line of battlements. In the XVIIth century during the Philippine dynasty, the defence system was completed with the Pico Castle and São Tiago Fortress. Construction of the São Lourenço Palace in the centre of the city, which has housed the island's governors for centuries, began in 1540 and was enlarged throughout the XVIth and XVIIth centuries. Nowadays the three fortresses are open to the public.

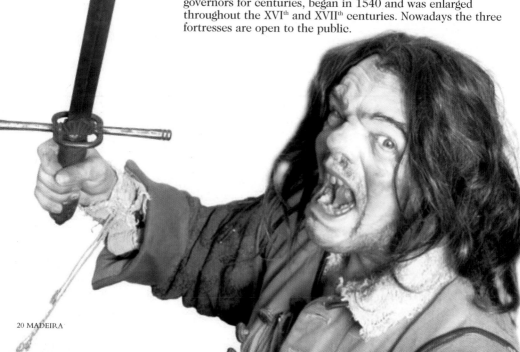

Fortaleza de S: João: do Pico
Na Ilha da Madeira

The unification of Iberia

AS A RESULT of the matrimonial alliances between Portugal and Castile and the absence of a direct heir to the Portuguese crown, the son of Emperor Charles V, Philip II of the House of Hapsburg, King of Spain and feudal lord of Flanders and Sicily amongst other territories, rose to the throne in 1580. The union of the two royal houses resulted in Portuguese territories being attacked by enemies of Spain such as France, England and Holland which were also disputing rights over the territories discovered and granted to the Iberian countries by the Pope. In 1540 a rebellion put the Duke of Bragança, the head of the most important noble family in Portugal, on the throne and Portugal once again became independent. It was at this time that the fortification of Funchal was completed.

The São João do Pico Fortress *according to a drawing by Bartolomeu João, the architect himself*

King Philip II *of Spain, Philip I of Portugal*

From sugar to wine

FOR SEVERAL centuries Madeira's economy was successively dominated by diverse export products. After a short period during which investment was made in wheat of which there was a shortage in Portugal, it was the turn of sugar which made Madeira famous. This was followed by wine which is almost certainly more renowned than the island itself. However, none of these products completely obscured the others. As the island depended excessively on imported food, whenever exports declined there was hunger. A farming culture with original features sprung up as a backdrop to this export economy.

"White gold"

WHEAT was the first large-scale crop which was exported to the mainland and Ceuta for some time – Portugal suffered from a chronic lack of cereals and this might have been one of the motives for colonising Madeira. Years later, in 1452, sugar cane was introduced. Exported to Rouen, Flanders, Genova, Venice, Constantinople and England, sugar from Madeira was widely appreciated throughout Europe. Around 1490 the sugar mills produced and exported almost 100,000 "arrobas" of sugar every year to the main trading centres of Europe (an "arroba" corresponded to around 15 kg.) The tax on sugar was a very important source of income for the feudal lord of Madeira and, later, for the crown. In the beginning African, Canarian and Moorish slaves were used for labour.

The slave population of Madeira accompanied the success of the sugar industry. In 1552 there were around 3,000 slaves living on the island. As from the middle of the XVIth century the Madeira sugar trade began to suffer competition from Brazil and the Antilles and sugar cane production gradually declined possibly also on account of the impoverishment of the land by this very demanding crop.

*A **Brazilian sugar mill** from the XVIIth century probably similar to the old Madeiran devices*

A Madeiran invention

EARLY SUGAR-MAKING technology used horizontal stone cylinders to crush the sugar cane. In 1452 Diogo de Teive built the first water mill in Madeira. There are records that suggest that up until 1494 there were at least 16 sugar mills driven by water on Madeira. Over time the stone cylinders were substituted by metal cylinders. Sugar-making technology from Madeira was introduced to São Tomé, Cape Verde and Brazil by experts from Madeira. The device with three vertical cylinders often found in Brazilian mills dating from the XVIIth century and West Indian mills from the XVIIIth century have been attributed to a Madeiran invention. Recent research shows that terms related to the sugar cane industry are similar in Madeira, Brazil and Cape Verde.

A sugar shield

THIS COAT OF ARMS
of the city of Funchal dates
from the XVIIth century and
represents five sugar moulds
laid out in a cross and two
sugar canes, demonstrating
the importance of this
product in Madeira's
economy. Later grapes and
vine leaves were added in
recognition of the
significance wine had
assumed in the meantime.

Sugar and Flemish art

THE EXPORT of sugar
to Flanders resulted in the
import of Flemish paintings
of religious inspiration,
facilitated by commercial
contacts. Many were
commissioned for private
churches or chapels. The
most important collection
is now in the Museum of
Sacred Art in Funchal.
Tradition has it that this
Flemish painting (Saint
Joaquim and Saint Anne)
from the Madalena Church
and now in the Museum was
commissioned by Henrique
Alemão and represents him
and his wife. Henrique
Alemão is an obscure
character, a mysterious
Knight of Saint Catherine
on whom Prince Henry the
Navigator bestowed land in
Madalena do Mar on the
southwest coast of Madeira
in 1457. It is said that in
fact he was a fugitive king,
Wladislaw III of Poland.

Vines on the north coast of the island

The origins of the wine

IN 1455 Alvise da Cà da Mosto (or Cadamosto), a Venetian navigator in the service of the Portuguese crown had already made mention of Madeira's "very good wines, really exceptionally good... in such quantity that they suffice the islanders and many are exported" and he makes special mention of Malmsey, a much appreciated grape variety which Prince Henry the Navigator ordered from Candia in Crete. Another Italian, Giulio Landi, who passed through Madeira in 1530 stated that the island

"also produces a large quantity of wine of all kinds but most are fortified white wines (...) as well as Malmsey, but in lesser quantities, which is reputed to be better than that from Candia. As the islanders do not usually drink wine, they sell it to merchants who take it to the Iberian Peninsular and other northern countries".

Towards the end of the XVIth century Madeira wine was certainly already famous in England. In Shakespeare's Henry IV (1597) Poins needles Falstaff interrogating

him as to the substance of the agreement by which he had sold his soul to the devil on Good Friday "for a cup of Madeira and cold capon's leg". Here is the passage in which Madeira wine is mentioned (Act I, Scene II):

Poins: Good morrow, sweet Hal. What says Monsieur Remorse? What says Sir John Sack and Sugar? Jack! How agrees the devil and thee about thy soul, that thou soldest him on Good-Friday last for a cup of Madeira and a cold capon's leg?

The "Anglo-Madeirans"

The Church of the Holy Trinity (*Igreja da Santíssima Trindade) was inaugurated in 1822. With unusual architecture attributed to Henry Veitch it cost 10 thousand pounds at the time, the equivalent to a million pounds today*

FROM THE MIDDLE of the XVIIth century wine substituted sugar as the main export product. The business attracted many foreign merchants, this time mostly English, who profited from trade agreements (such as the Methuen Treaty of 1703) according to which Portuguese wines benefited from a reduction in customs duties – this also led to the boom in the Port wine trade. The British Navigation Acts published from 1660 onwards obliged all merchandise destined for English colonies to be loaded in England onto ships flying the English flag. But Madeira was an exception and English ships took on supplies of wine here on their way to the vast British empire especially to the Antilles and North America which became the main markets for Madeira wine. A cemetery was also built in 1802 and, finally, the Anglican Church of the Holy Trinity was inaugurated in 1822 in Rua do Quebra Costas, serving the circa 700 Britons then resident on the island. The British presence in Madeira became more marked with its occupation by English troops between 1801 and 1802 with a view to preventing invasion by the French. Between 1807 and 1814 the archipelago fell under British administration during the Peninsular Wars and the transferral of the Portuguese court and government to Rio de Janeiro. By means of their family businesses the British community continued to play a very important role in Madeira's economy throughout the XIXth and XXth centuries with involvement in many areas of business. The families always retained their British nationality and culture throughout the generations. When recently questioned as to where he belonged, a distinguished member of the British community in Madeira stated:" We're Anglo-Madeirans".

A shaft and screw wine press from the album Recollections of Madeira *by W.S. Pitt Springett, circa 1843. This ancient type of press was common on the island until the 1980's*

"Canteiro" and "estufa" wines

AFTER Malmsey other grape varieties such as Verdelho, Bual, Sercial and Terrantez were introduced. These are known as the five noble grape varieties of Madeira wine as opposed to the American varieties which appeared later. For centuries the must was produced in Roman style, or shaft and screw, wine presses with the grapes being trodden by foot; after this the remains would be placed under a shaft (a thick beam) and pressure was increased by suspending a weight that was raised by turning a screw which fitted into the shaft.

Fermentation is halted by the addition of brandy which results in the presevation of part of the grape sugar and increases the alcoholic content (similarly to other fortified wines such as Port). The traditional ageing process was and is called "canteiro"; this requires casks to be placed in storage with little ventilation where relatively high temperatures can be achieved. This process produces a very aromatic wine with an exceptional longevity – hence its suitability for long journeys. In fact Madeira wine may be kept in good condition for one or two hundred years without loosing its quality.

At the end of the XVIIIth century Madeira wine exporters began to notice that the wine which was shipped to India but not sold had improved on its return as if it had aged faster due to the high temperatures to which it was subjected when travelling through the tropics. From then on they began to produce "vinho da roda" which was sent especially on a return trip to India. Shortly afterwards there were producers who decided to reproduce the process on land, placing casks in "estufas" heated by steam at high temperatures – this gave rise to the second kind of vinification, "estufa" wines, generally considered of lesser quality than "canteiro" wines.

The letters of William Bolton

ONE of the most important merchants at the turn of the XVIIth century was William Bolton who exported wine and citrus preserves to the British colonies in the West Indies and North America. He imported fabrics and clothing, cereals and other food from places as diverse as the Azores and Ireland, England and North America. His commercial correspondence has been preserved and is a precious testament as to how a businessman of that time was able to manage an impressive number of contacts, dispatching and receiving merchandise and payments on both sides of the Atlantic. Bolton also mentions events such as Edmund Halley's passage through Madeira "on his way to the Brazilian coast and south of the Cape in order to study the deviation of the compass".

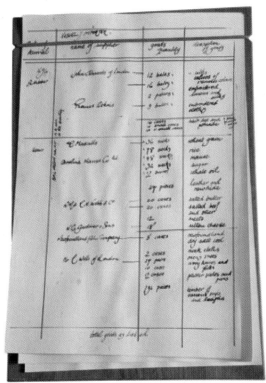

Business is business. Duplicates of letters were sent on various ships to guard against loss. In one letter dated April 1696 there is mention of the conspiracy against William III of England. In another from 1699 Bolton philosophises that "when business is bad it must get better"

A tradição mantém-se

FOLLOWING the decline provoked by the plagues of oidium and phyloxera which so affected the European grape varieties as from the second half of the XIXth century and the abuse of the "estufa" system, Madeira wine has recovered its quality standards and prestige over the last decades. This was aided by the creation of the Madeira Wine Institute (1979) which established strict rules regarding the obligatory quantity of European grape varieties and the classification of types of wine, prohibited the export of bulk wine and created incentives for the production European grape varieties; adhesion to the European Union reinforced this initiative. Of the producers of British origin there is still the Madeira Wine Company which today belongs to the Blandy and Symington groups (the latter being an important producer of Port wine) and sells historic labels such as Blandy's, Cossart Gordon, Leacock and Miles, accounting for around a third of the market. Other prestigious producers include Artur Barros e Sousa, Barbeito, Justino Henriques and Henriques & Henriques.

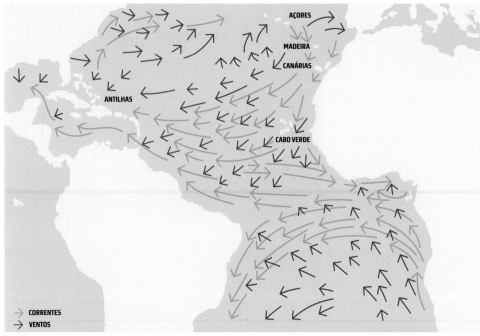

The predominant winds over the Atlantic are such that all sailing boats going to the Americas, Caribbean, Southern Africa and Indian Ocean pass by Madeira or the Canaries. The return journey is made via the Azores

A crossroad in the Atlantic

THANKS to its location Funchal was an important supply point on the routes to Africa, India, the Antilles and the Americas. For vessels under sail the sea route to all these destinations always goes via Madeira or the Canaries, which are reached with the northeast trade winds. From here ships continue south to the latitude of Cape Verde where the predominant winds blow from the east; close to the South American coast the route forks, leading to the Antilles and North America or to South America, Southern Africa and the Indian Ocean. These routes are still used by leisure boats today.

The ship-spotting towers

THROUGHOUT the XVIIIth and XIXth centuries Funchal merchants and house owners constructed two types of properties: the "quintas" with houses surrounded by lush gardens on the outskirts of Funchal and the palatial houses in the centre of the city with several floors and the characteristic ship-spotting towers which permitted movement in the port to be observed.

*XVIIIth century palace in Rua do Bispo, Funchal, with a **ship-spotting tower***

A navigational challenge

DESPITE its importance the port of Funchal was known for being quite tricky. Sheltered from the predominant winds from the north it could nevertheless be very dangerous for shipping when there were winds from the south. The islet in front of Funchal aided the approach. Funchal had no docks or quay so ships anchored in the bay. Cargo and passengers were transferred to smaller rowing boats which transported them to dry land. However, bad weather could force ships to anchor up to 500 metres away from the shore. In violent storms captains used to take shelter close to Ponta da Oliveira in Caniço. During the XVIIth century a fort was constructed on the islet to

Funchal. From the book A Voyage to Conchinchina, in the Years 1792 and 1793 *by John Barrow*

protect ships from attack. The building of the port began in 1770 but the stretch of mole leading to the Nª. Sª. da Conceição

Fortress was only finished in 1878. In the XXth century the mole was extended twice in 1933 and 1960.

James Cook and the Endeavour

CAPTAIN COOK and the crew of the Endeavour anchored off Funchal on 12th September 1768 to take on board basic provisions including 3,300 gallons of wine. The expedition's scientists undertook various studies on Madeira during their stay. Cook and his men were en route to Tahiti on the orders of the Royal Society. Their mission was to record Venus' trajectory in relation to the sun which was calculated on 3rd June 1769. Cook had also been commissioned to look for a "continent to the south". This was the first voyage

to be well equipped as a biological expedition. Led by Sir Joseph Banks, it included astronomers, naturalists and artists who assembled botanical, zoological and ethnological records during the expedition. Records of the flora of Madeira were drawn by Sydney Parkinson. On his return John Hawksworth used Banks' and Parkinson's diaries to compile observations and a description of the voyage.

The Endeavour. On his first voyage Captain Cook's ship was a collier which was called the Earl of Pembroke. During its refurbishment and refitting in 1768 it was renamed the Endeavour

The troubled XIXth century

THE XIXTH CENTURY had barely dawned when the island was occupied by British troops on account of tense relations with revolutionary France. Later, after the invasion of Portugal by Napoleon's armies in 1807 and the flight of the royal family and Portuguese elite to Brazil, the island came under English administration until the defeat of the French on the Portuguese mainland in 1814. In practice Madeira became incorporated into the commercial network of the British Empire, reinforcing the power of the English merchants who were therefore able to export their wines freely to Great Britain and the whole empire including America. As from the middle of the century Madeira suffered a series of agricultural, social and religious crises which resulted in mass emigration and economic changes.

Interior of "Venda" in Serra de Santo António from the album "Recollections of Madeira" by W.S. Pitt Springett, circa 1843

Floods

WITH a torrential regime (large and sometimes sudden changes in the volume of water) Madeira's rivers can be a destructive force to be contended with, bursting their banks while dragging away large blocks of stone – and everything in their way – in the flood.

The biggest flood ever occurred on 9th October 1803. After several days of intense rain the rivers burst their banks in various places all over the island and especially violently in Funchal. The Santa Maria quarter was particularly affected with roads and whole buildings dragged into the sea by the fury of Ribeira de João Gomes. Santa Maria do Calhau Church, the oldest on the island, (located to the south of today's market) was badly damaged and finally demolished in 1835. 600 people are estimated to have died. After this tragedy a military engineer of French origin, Brigadier Oudinot, who had already been working Portugal for some years was sent to Madeira. Oudinot ordered walls to

A Ribeira de Santa Luzia. Gravura de Frank Dillon, cerca de 1850

be built alongside Funchal's three riverbeds, assuming the aspect they have today. Despite these defences floods continue to do damage every now and again.

On 20 February 2010, *a new catastrophe occurred. In Funchal, as in 1993, flooding brought chaos to the river banks and filled the lower part of the city with mud.*

Oidium and phyloxera

AS HAD also been the case in other European wine regions, a fungus called oidium devastated the Madeira vineyards from1852 onwards. A remedy was quickly found – spraying the vines with sulphur. 1872 saw another plague of European proportions but this time much worse – phyloxera,

an insect of American origin which attacks the roots of the vines. The area covered by vineyards was drastically diminished. By 1883 phyloxera had reduced the area planted with vines to a fifth of its original size. Another consequence was the almost total disappearance of the European grape

varieties. The solution found was to plant American vines which were immune to phyloxera to serve as root stock for grafting European varieties. In the meantime many producers chose to produce wine directly from the American vines resulting in a decline in quality.

An island of emigrants

EMIGRATION began in the XVIIIth century with movements organised and financed by the Crown to colonise regions in the south of Brazil; however, it really took off as from the mid XIXth century on account of over-population and was prompted in particular by various crises such as the religious disturbances associated to the Protestant movement led by Father Robert Kalley and the oidium (1852) and phylloxera (1872) catastrophes. Between 1834 and 1871 around 55 thousand emigrants left Madeira. During the XIXth century the main destinations were Demerara in British Guiana, Suriname in the Antilles (Jamaica, Trinidad, and St. Kitts), Brazil and Hawaii where emigrants from Madeira were responsible for the introduction of what today is considered a traditional musical instrument, the ukulele. Over the last decades of the XIXth century and most of the XXth century large scale emigration from Madeira continued. Nowadays the largest Madeiran communities can be found in South Africa (around 350 thousand Madeirans and their descendants), Venezuela (200 thousand), Brazil (150 thousand), United States (50 thousand), Australia (30 thousand) and Canada (20 thousand). Extraordinary figures considering that the resident population of Madeira is only 250 thousand people. From the last decades of the XXth century onwards emigration fell sharply assuming a seasonal character, the main destinations being Switzerland and the Channel Islands (Jersey and Guernsey). The economic situation at the beginning of the twenty-first century caused emigration from Madeira to rise again.

PARA A PROVINCIA DE S. PAULO
BRAZIL 8

E' sperado o vapor **FRANK-FURT** que sàe de Bremen a 24 do corrente para conduzir passageiros para a provincia de S. Paulo.

Dão-se passagens gratuitas a familias que queiram ir para a-quella provincia principalmen-te dedicarem-se à agricultura.

Não ha contracto algum: os emigrantes são completamente livres para escolherem colloca-ção e se empregarem aonde me-lhor lhes convier sem terem de pagar indemnização alguma

Trata-se no escriptorio de E-duardo de Freitas &. C.ª, rua da Alfandega n.° 14.

(50)

*This 1886 advertisement in the **Diário de Notícias** da Madeira offers free passage to emigrants to Brazil, reflecting the atmoshpere of crisis*

Napoleon, Consul Veitch and 1792 Madeira

TAKEN PRISONER by the English and forced into exile on the Island of Saint Helena, Napoleon stopped in Funchal in August 1815 on board the Northumberland where he was visited by the then British consul in Madeira, Henry Veitch. The story goes that Veitch made a gaffe by calling the ex-emperor "Your Majesty" when offering his services. Napoleon asked for fruit and books and Veitch sent him a gift which included a cask of 1792 Madeira wine. However, Napoleon had been forbidden to drink by his doctors so the cask was not opened; it was bought and returned to Madeira where the wine was used to make a lot called Battle of

Waterloo. When Winston Churchill visited Madeira in 1950 he was given a bottle of this wine which he insisted on serving to his guests himself with the words "Do you realise that when this wine was made Marie Antoinette was still alive?" Henry Veitch was a very prosperous wine merchant who left his mark on Madeira on account of the various houses he had built amongst which special mention goes to the enormous residence in Funchal in Rua 5 de Outubro which now houses the Madeira Wine Institute, Quinta do Jardim da Serra, nowadays a hotel, and Quinta Calaça, today's Clube Naval.

Napoleon on board the Bellerophon (the ship from which he was transferred to the Northumberland on which he travelled to his exile in Saint Helena). Painting by William Quiller Orchardson

Robert Reid Kally, the Calvinist missionary

LIKE many others at the time, the wealthy Scottish doctor, Robert Kalley (1809--1888), arrived in Madeira in 1838 in search of the benefits of the climate for his wife who had tuberculosis. This was the beginning of an extraordinary adventure. Shocked by the poverty, illiteracy and ignorance of the Bible among the peasants of Madeira, Kalley decided to offer free medical services and teach reading and writing while preaching from Portuguese versions of the Bible which he imported from England and distributed for free at a time when Catholics only had access to the Bible in Latin. He set up a small hospital and various primary schools. Thanks to all this he became increasingly popular while also attracting suspicion from the social and ecclesiastical elite. As from 1841 problems arose with the Bishop of Funchal banning Kalley's "religious speeches" followed by petitions to support the Scottish doctor; in 1943 the Bibles he spread around the island were prohibited and meetings in his house were forbidden with police

*The famous **Fernandes** rum from Trinidad is produced by descendants of Protestant refugees from Madeira*

stationed at his front door to prevent the Portuguese from entering. 1846 saw the enforced closure of the schools set up by Kalley and legal action taken against his followers, some of whom were condemned to death for heresy. During this year his house was stormed by a crowd. Kalley took refuge at the British consulate and, dressed as a woman, he fled the island for America. A large number of his supporters followed in his footsteps. Many of them went to Trinidad in the Antilles where today some surnames can still be found; some of these are connected to the production of rum; others went to Illinois in the United States where Kalley settled and managed to receive an indemnity from the Portuguese government for the assault on his house. In 1855 Kalley went to Brazil where he was one of the pioneers of Protestantism. The British director, Sam Mendes (American Beauty), is a descendant of Protestant families from Madeira who took refuge in Trinidad after this episode.

Sugar cane harvest

The resurgence of sugar

IN THE WAKE of the plagues which blighted the vines, sugar cane made a strong comeback. From an insignificant quantity at the beginning of the XIXth century sugar production rose to almost 275 tonnes in 1854 and 528 tonnes in 1871, continuing to increase until World War II after which it gradually declined. The rebirth of the industry is partly due to the adoption of new industrial methods with special mention going to a British family, the Hintons, who dominated the market. On account of the lack of wine an excessive consumption of brandy gave rise to concerns about alcoholism. The large Hinton factory in Funchal (known as the "engenho do Hinton") closed its doors in 1986. Today three small mills remain: one in Ribeiro Seco in Funchal which only produces honey and the ones in Calheta and Porto da Cruz which make honey and brandy, the latter only for domestic consumption.

"Poncha"

BRANDY production combined with a shortage of wine resulted in the widespread consumption of brandy. A traditional drink, "poncha", dates from this period – brandy diluted with water, lemon and sugar or honey, today made in many more varieties.

Football

IT WAS Harry Hinton from the second generation of the family who organised the first game of football in Portugal at Achada, Camacha, in 1875. The famous footballer Cristiano Ronaldo was born in Funchal, in Santo António. The first club that he played with was Andorinha.

New Industries

*The old factory of the **Companhia Insular da Madeira** in Largo do Pelourinho, Funchal*

THE SECOND HALF of the XIXth and beginning of the XXth centuries saw the development of other industries such as the flour mills concentrated between the Ribeira de João Gomes and Ribeira de Santa Luzia in downtown Funchal. The large factories which constituted an industrial area in the middle of the town can still be seen today.

In the drinks sector the first beer and soft drinks factory emerged in 1872 – the Atlantic Brewery – which, in 1935, merged with other manufacturers and became the Empresa de Cervejas da Madeira. The service sector also prospered with the development of tourism. The introduction of steam ships permitted not only coastal navigation around the island but also the emergence of the business of supplying coal to ships and a shipyard. The dairy industry was another area which prospered during this time, especially butter, most of which was exported. Companies with British origins connected to the wine trade were involved in all these industries.

The last commercial crop

THE LAST important commercial crop in Madeira was the banana which flourished from 1925 onwards on the lower, sunnier slopes in the west of the island where it gradually replaced sugar cane. At the end of the XXth century there were still banana trees in the very centre of Funchal. Proof of the profitability of this crop is that, at the beginning of the XXIth century, banana trees can still be seen on land with a high commercial value for construction on the seafront in the western part of Funchal.

José Silvestre Ribeiro

HAVING reached Madeira in 1846 accompanying an envoy from the Portuguese government sent to deal with the religious crisis linked to Robert Kalley, an old soldier from the Liberal Wars, José Silvestre Ribeiro, was to remain as governor until 1852. The following year he had to deal with a starvation crisis because of the plague which attacked the potato crop (the same which caused the tragedy in Ireland a few years before); he was responsible for various public works such as the establishment of a network of shelters (an example of which can be seen today in the Casa de Abrigo do Poiso destined to shelter travellers between Funchal and the north of the island), the bridge over Ribeiro Seco and Estrada Monumental. Ribeiro was also the first to incentivate the embroidery industry in an attempt to reduce the economic crisis provoked by the mildew and oidium plagues that attacked the vines.

The Count of Carvalhal

ANTÓNIO Leandro da Câmara Carvalhal Esmeraldo Atouguia Bettencourt de Sá Machado (1831-1888), 2nd Count of Carvalhal, is a symbol of the greatness and decadence of those who inherited by entailment. He inherited vast properties – including that which had belonged to João Esmeraldo during the XVIth century – which made him the island's biggest landowner and one of the richest men in Portugal during his time. To assess his fortune you just have to remember that he owned the São Pedro Palace (the current Funchal Municipal Library and Museum) and Quinta do Palheiro. He used to live in Lisbon where he kept company with the intellectuals of the era – writers such as Garrett and Herculano. Spending vast sums of money between Funchal, Lisbon, Madrid and Paris, his fortune dis not withstand his bohemian habits. He ended up ruined and obliged to sell off his properties.

*The **S. Pedro Palace** bears witness to the opulence of the Carvalhal family in their heyday*

Solutions for the crisis

ON THE INITIATIVE of the governor, José Silvestre Ribeiro, an industrial exhibition took place in Funchal in 1850; embroidery was one of the products exhibited. It was such a success that it was repeated within the London Universal Exhibition a year later.

An English citizen, Elizabeth Phelps, played an important role in promoting Madeira embroidery in London and she undertook the first exports as well as starting embroidery schools. Shortly the embroidery reached the United States and then Germany. In 1862 a little over one thousand embroiderers were registered; this figure rose to 30 thousand in 1902 and 60 thousand in 1962 at the peak of this industry. From 1880 to World War I German merchants dominated embroidery exports followed by the Syrians until the 1930's.

The willows of Camacha

TRADITIONALLY Funchal merchants would buy willows, already boiled and peeled, on the north coast of the island where they were more abundant; these would then be given to artisans, usually in Camacha, who made baskets and furniture. This, in turn, would return to the merchants who would have it varnished and export it mostly to the United States and mainland Portugal. As from the middle of the XXth century this industry gave in to competition from other countries and today production is limited to the island market for sale to tourists or locals. Camacha continues to be the centre of production.

The peasants of Madeira

ANONYMOUS protagonists of history, the Madeiran peasants were the creators of a rural landscape deeply marked by man, over the years producing not only commercial crops for export but also crops for subsistence or sale on the local market. Madeira's rural world has very particular characteristics. The very steep terrain obliged the

Wheat harvest in São Paulo, Ribeira Brava

construction of terraces – called "poios" in Madeira – with stone walls to prevent the soil being washed away by water. Sometimes the walls were built on bare rock, earth from other places being brought in to fill the "poio". All this implies heavy maintenance work.

The "colonia"

The use of a hammock (also called a palanquim *when the framework was made of steel) accentuates the contrast between the well-to-do classes and the peasants. The passenger in the picture is Robert Reid Kalley*

Society in Madeira was divided between two extremes – the landowners and merchants who lived in Funchal and the peasants. Perhaps on account of the need for heavy labour to create agricultural land a peculiar form of rural landownership was developed – the "colonia". The contract for the "colonia" between the landowner and the peasant who farmed it – the tenant – was enduring and hereditary; the tenant was obliged to give the landlord half his harvest. All improvements – walls, houses etc. remained the property of the tenant. If the landowner wanted to reclaim his land and terminate the contract he was obliged to pay an indemnity to the tenant for the improvements. The improvements and the land farmed by the tenant were divided between his heirs. On the other hand, many of the landlords inherited by entailment – the land was inherited by the eldest son and could not be sold. As a result property was concentrated amongst the few and farms became fragmented. In 1863 the entailment system was abolished in Portugal. As a result of this and also of the reduction in agricultural income and money coming from those who had emigrated, the peasants began to buy land. However, the "colonia" remained in existence throughout the XXth century and was officially abolished in 1977.

Shepherds on Pico do Areeiro (1966). *The livestock (goats and pigs) was left to roam on the hills and was then herded by shepherds.*

Terraces *("poios") in Ribeira da Janela, Porto Moniz*

The taming of the hills

THE DIFFICULTIES inherent to the lie of the land in Madeira led to the construction of a rural landscape profoundly marked by man; this is characterised by terracing locally known as "poios" up to an altitude of 700 metres and by the irrigation system; the multi-crop regime is intensive except in the cases of banana trees and sugar cane with various crops such as potato, sweet potato, beans, cabbage, maize and even wheat on higher land, co-existing on the same piece of land. Around one quarter of the island's total surface used to be farmed. With the destruction of the forest to create farmland from the time of the first settlement, the land, on account of its gradient, was often washed away by rain; consequently supporting walls, often with protruding stones that serve as steps, were constructed. Terraces made this way create small parcels of land on which it is not possible to use a plough or animals with the result that farms, already small in their own right, are even more fragmented. On account of the influence of the altitude on the temperature, humidity and rain, crops are laid out in layers – sugar cane or banana trees, vines, food crops, forests, cork oak groves and high altitude pastures.

Almost vegetarian

THE PEASANTS were obliged to produce a commercial crop such as wine or sugar cane and at the same time grow their subsistence crops. They also often kept a pig or a cow. Cows were reared in cowsheds where their bedding was made from ferns. Once saturated with cow dung this bedding served as fertiliser. The cow produced milk for sale in Funchal or to the dairy factories. There was also livestock – goat and pigs – which ran loose and had to be "hunted down" on the hills.

"Levadas", the water highways

THERE IS abundant water in Madeira which means there are hardly any crops which go without irrigation. The greater the altitude the more it rains and the greater number of water sources there are. And on the north coast it rains much more than on the south. From the early days of colonisation water was sourced in the mountains and taken by means of watercourses – "levadas" – to the agricultural land. "Levadas" follow an almost flat route. Other descending channels branch off them taking the water to the land. Water distribution is overseen by "levadeiros" who open and close the sluice gates so that the water reaches its destination. Each usufructuary is allocated a set period of time of water every so many days; this is known as the "giro da água". The timing of the "giro" changes and may fall at any time of the day or night – sometimes this implies waking up in the middle of the night to direct the water across the land. The oldest "levadas" are on the south coast and are managed by associations of usufructuaries called "heréus". As from the middle of the XIXth century the state began to build several "levadas" which were much longer than the old ones and take water from the mountains on the north side to be sold to farmers all over the island.

*During the **1940's and 1950's** a new network of "levadas" was built significantly increasing irrigation capacity and including hydro-electric power generation. Construction often involved dramatic conditions as illustrated by this image*

Levada do Norte, Perestrellos Photographos, 1950's

A single-storey rural house with a four-sided roof and next to it a cowshed. Some thatched houses are constructed in a similar way to this cowshed

Traditional houses

IN THE EARLY DAYS of colonialism the modest houses must have built from wood with thatched rooves. Over time houses with three or four-sided rooves, wooden or stone walls began to substitute these in some parts of the island; some of these had only one room with the kitchen in a separate building. Nowadays there are very few left. Another kind of rural house, much more common today, has a four-sided roof and one or two storeys, the upper floor being used for living in and the lower floor (the "loja") as a cellar and storeroom; often each floor has separate entrances. Many houses have roofing finishes with allegorical figures such as doves or boys' heads. The green shutters which guard against the light are almost omnipresent; often they have a tilting section allowing the slats to be turned providing a discreet view of the street and those passing by without fully opening the shutter. Another common feature are the seats built into the walls of the property overlooking the street and latticed pergolas.

*Replicas of **traditional houses** in Santana*

Madeiran dress

"wearing traditional island dress which nowadays [1853-1854] is rare. The outfit consists of a bodice of yellow corduroy embroidered in white with a snow-white shirt pleated and fastened around the neck. The shoulders are only covered by the shirt's short sleeves which leave the arms bare. The skirt, short and loose-fitting, is made from the rough wollen fabric called "seriguilha"; it may be blue, dark brown or striped red, blue, white and yellow. The hair is parted at the front and secured at the back in a bun; a blue cloth cap lined with red and common to both sexes is worn on top of the head at an angle. Nowadays the usual dress is made from printed cotton which has faded to off white." One of the few pieces of typical Madeiran dress which can still be seen today are the so--called "barretes de orelhas" (cap with ear flaps) made of wool with protection for the ears and a tassel on top.

ACCORDING to XIXth century witnesses Madeiran peasants used to wear a shirt, jacket, wide linen breeches and boots. The women wore striped skirts made from a linen and wool fabric, a blue or red cape and flat boots. The outfit was completed by a cap with a pointed tip which looked like an upside funnel. This cap must have appeared in the XIXth century and later

disappeared. This is how the peasants painted by English landscape painters such as Picken or Frank Dillon appear. Isabella de França mentions having met a peasant woman

The difficulties of transport

UNTIL the advent of roads and motorcars, getting around the island was quite complicated. The most common form of transport was on foot, by horse or hammock according to social status. Merchandise was transported by sledge, a kind of cart without wheels, pulled by bullocks. A single network of roads laid with stones covered the whole island, crossing from north to south at Encumeada (1007 m), Poiso (1412 m) and Portela (592 m). Sometimes the gradient was so steep that the road became steps. Coastal shipping played an important role both in the transport of passengers and of goods since it was often much simpler to go from one point on the coast to another by sea rather than by land. As from the second half of the XIXth century and up to World War I a series of quays were built permitting the journey round the island to be made by sea. The last of these regular boats, which used to run between Funchal and Paúl da Serra, stopped working towards the end of the 1970's.

The Gavião, a famous boat on the round-the-island run during the first half of the XXth century

The Casa de Abrigo do Poiso was built in 1850 by João Silvestre Ribeiro. It was meant to be used as a shelter for travellers between Funchal and the north coast in an area where the cold often claimed mortal victims. Today it is a restaurant

The tourism era

IN THE XVIIITH CENTURY Madeira's climate became renowned for its mild winters and supposed therapeutic virtues in treating tuberculosis. This was the beginning of tourism on the island with wealthy people from the north of Europe coming to spend the winter. The first travel guides published at the beginning of the XIXth century focus on medical and climatic considerations. But the island revealed itself to be much more than that. In the heyday of the romantic taste for travel, exoticism and landscapes, Madeira was quite an exotic island with spectacular landscapes – and quite close to the European continent. Madeira's charms were disseminated by means of albums of prints made by English artists. Madeira Illustrated (1840) with landscapes by Andrew Picken accompanied by texts on the climate, health and history, is a classic. Tourists often stayed in private houses and some of the intermediaries later launched themselves into building hotels. In 1840 there were only two hotels, in 1891, fourteen. With the decline of the illness and the discovery of treatments for tuberculosis health ceased to be Madeira's main attraction and the guides stop mentioning it. Up until the 1960's tourism grew slowly before moving into a boom: 2,295 beds in 1967, 12,244 in 1982 and around 20 thousand at the turn of the XXIst century.

*A young English aristocrat, Lady Prudence Jellicoe, showing off her diving skills at **Reid's Hotel** on the cover of a British magazine in 1932*

Isabella's journal

One of the best travel books on Madeira remained unpublished for over one hundred years. Journal of a Visit to Madeira and Portugal 1853-1854 *by Isabella de França was only published in Funchal in 1970 in English and Portuguese.*

Illustrations from **Journal of a Visit to Madeira and Portugal, 1853-1854**

The way up to Monte

"Madam must be patient" – *Road to Curral*

Lazareto

Embarking at Calheta

THIS MANUSCRIPT was found by a Madeiran collector in a second-hand bookshop in London during the 1930's. It was later discovered that it had been written and illustrated by an English lady called Isabella who was married to José Henrique (Joseph Henry as he liked to sign his name) de França, a London merchant of Madeiran origin and heir to entailed estate on the island. Although their trip to Madeira was their honeymoon Isabella was not exactly young – she was already 57 and her husband 50. In the journal which she probably intended to publish since there are various references to "my readers", Isabella de França is revealed as an accomplished writer, sensitive and attentive to all details – she is enchanted by the island's landscapes, she enjoys the peculiarities of Madeira society, she is intrigued by the people's habits and dress. She also proves herself to be skilful with watercolours with a capacity for recording details in an almost photographic style.

Strange modes of transport

Some of the tourist attractions which appeared during the XIXth century were adaptations of traditional forms of transport: bullock carts adapted from the sledges which used to transport goods and which continued to be used until the 1970's and hammocks, originally destined to transport the sick and the wealthy. The Monte toboggans, which used to make, and still do make, the journey between this summer resort with it its romantic hotels and high society "quintas" and Funchal, were set up in 1846. The Monte Railway, which made for a more comfortable and faster journey, was inaugurated in 1893 and worked until 1943.

*The **train** between Funchal and Monte ran between 1893 and 1943. Next to it a **toboggan**. Bottom left, a **bullock cart** used for sightseeing. Bottom right, a "**corça**" (sledge) piled with sugar cane outside Reid's Hotel*

Royal legends

DURING the XIXth century and much of the XXth century Madeira retained its aura of exclusive, aristocratic tourism. Some of the personalities who assed through or lived here became legends on the island. This is not quite the case of Empress Elizabeth of Austria, also known as Sissi (1838-1897) who stayed at a *quinta* then known as Quinta Vigia (no longer in existence) in 1860 and also in 1891, this time at the recently inaugurated Reid's Palace Hotel. In fact Sissi was a legend during her lifetime which ended tragically when she was assassinated by an anarchist. A legend which was revived during the 1950's on account of the enormous success of the series of films in which Ronny Schneider plays the young and beautiful empress with a difficult marriage and famous lovers. Charles I, the last emperor of Austro--Hungary, came to Madeira in 1922 and stayed at

Quinta do Monte. He died the same year, a victim of pneumonia, and is buried in the Nossa Senhora do Monte Church. Charles I enjoyed a completely different kind of fame after

his death: he was beatified in 2004 by Pope John Paul II on account of his efforts to establish peace during World War I; a miracle in 1960 confirmed his beatification.

Winston Churchill's short holidays

Winston Churchill was one of the most famous people ever to visit Madeira, a real living legend with the aura of the great vanquisher of World War II still very fresh. He came with his wife, Clementine, and his daughter, Diana, at the beginning of January 1950 intending to spend several months relaxing on the island, painting and writing the fourth volume of his war memories. He stayed at Reid's, visited the island in a Rolls Royce lent by a member of the British community – the story goes that its boot was turned into a bar – and painted watercolours in Câmara de Lobos as can be seen in the above photograph, one of the few taken during his stay. Unfortunately, the then British Labour prime minister, Clement Atlee, thought it would be a good idea to make the most of the historic Conservative leader's absence to call early elections and Churchill returned immediately to England on 12th January to lead the Tory campaign.

The Empress of Austria on the cover of the newspaper Le Petit Journal

Reid's, a legendary hotel

DURING THE 1880's a Scot, William Reid, bought a plot of land on cliff overlooking the sea on what was then the western outskirts of Funchal with the view to building a luxury hotel. Reid came to Madeira in 1836 and, having worked in the wine trade, he became an agent letting "quintas" to tourists; he then became a hotelier, the owner of three hotels in 1850. He did not live to see Reid's Palace Hotel completed and the hotel was inaugurated by his sons, William and Alfred. An immediate success, that very year it received the first of a long list of celebrities, the Empress of Austria, Sissi. Over the next years the hotel hosted Captain Scott on his way to Antartica, King Edward VII of England, George Bernard Shaw and Nobel Physics Prize winner and inventor of the wireless telegraph, Guglielmo Marconi, amongst many other famous people. In 1936 the hotel was bought by the Blandy family. Modernised and enlarged it re-opened after the end of World War II. It was recently sold to the Orient Express chain. With a magnificent location – it is difficult to imagine better – lush gardens and a comfortable and discreet décor, Reid's became a classic in the luxury hotel market, a kind of Madeiran ideal which still retains its discreet charm today.

*The **Reid's Guest Book** contains the signatures of many celebrities, aristocrats, millionaires and members of the jet-set including Winston Churchill, Guglielmo Marconi, Princess Stephanie of Monaco and Bette Midler*

Reid's at the end of the XIXth century when it was still called Reid's New Hotel

The World Wars

*The French ship, **Kangaroo**, sunk by a German torpedo in the Bay of Funchal in 1916*

PORTUGUESE participation in World War I resulted in a high death toll in the Belgian trenches. Apart from sporadic attacks on ships of the allied nations, Funchal was bombarded by a German submarine on 3rd and 12th December 1917. Madeira also suffered on account of interrupted supplies and the absence of tourists. In World War II Portugal remained neutral and the skilful diplomacy of the dictator Salazar even enabled the country to profit from it. In Madeira, however, the decline in shipping in the Funchal port had serious consequences, paralysing imports of food as well as exports and hindering tourism. Rationing was necessary and migration to Brazil was promoted with lotteries for free passages. However, it was during his time that the most important public works were undertaken, for example, Avenida do Mar and Avenida do Infante as well as public buildings such as the Mercado dos Lavradores amongst several others.

The Gibraltan ladies

FOR MANY in Madeira the Second World War years remained associated to some good memories. Following the bombing of Gibraltar the British decided to evacuate the population. One of the destinations chosen was Madeira, which, in July and August 1940, received around 2 thousand people, mostly female. In a city paralysed by a decline in tourism and unemployment, the Gibraltan ladies were an immediate success, filling the cafés and shops. The city came back to life. In an environment as conservative as Funchal where,to preserve their reputation, women did not go out alone it was astonishing to see women who smoked, went to cafés alone and took the sun on the Avenida benches. The Gibraltan ladies caused general excitement, particularly amongst the men. Some of them married in Madeira.

Cutting from the Diário de Notícias *da Madeira, 22-7-1940*

Flying in style

The first planes to bring passengers to Madeira operated between Southampton and Funchal where they used to land in the middle of the bay.

AQUILA AIRWAYS offered a first class service in keeping with the standards of the time when flying was a luxury; there were two weekly flights from Southampton to Funchal via Lisbon. The return ticket cost around 87 pounds, the equivalent to 1,714 pounds today. Founded by Barry Aikman, an ex-RAF World War II pilot, with Short Sutherland bombers adapted to transport passengers, Aquila began to operate this route, its first, in March 1949. The following decade the company bought other second-hand planes – Short Solents – from the same manufacturer and began to fly to other destinations such as Las Palmas and Capri. Aquila only flew until 1958 due to the lack of spare parts and a crash on the Isle of Wight which had a negative effect on confidence in the company. A Portuguese company, ARTOP, also flew seaplanes to Madeira in 1958 but it folded following an accident during the same year. In the meantime, the Porto Santo airport was inaugurated in 1960 and passengers for Madeira made the crossing from this island by boat. The Madeira airport in Santa Cruz was finally inaugurated in 1964.

AQUILA

*This seaplane was often used by Aquila Airways between Southampton and Madeira. A storm caused serious damage to the **City of Funchal** in Santa Margherita in Italy. It was withdrawn in October 1956*

CITY OF FUNCHAL

AQUILA AIRWAYS LIMITED

PASSENGER COUPON

5615

A Funchal-Lisbon return ticket, 1950

Discovering Madeira today

AFTER THIS SHORT journey through the history of Madeira we would like to make some suggestions for discovering Madeira today. You may get an idea of how Funchal used to be in the XVIIIth and XIXth centuries by taking a look at certain parts of the city; visiting the XVIIth century fortresses; walking along the "levadas", which have irrigated the island's fields for centuries, and the old walking trails; enjoying the Laurissilva forest, a living relic which exists in no other place in this dimension; eating ancient specialities such as "espetada" (meat skewers) with "bolo do caco" (local bread) at the "arraiais" (street festivals) to the sound of genuinely traditional music.

Quinta do Palheiro Ferreiro, Funchal

The ancient forest

Vendas Novas, São Jorge

THE LAURISSILVA forest is a natural relic, a kind of forest which in the past abounded in Europe and succumbed to the low temperatures of the Wurm ice age that came to an end around 10 thousand years BC. It is mostly composed of laurel trees and also of other trees from the same family ("til" (fetid laurel), "barbusano" (Canary laurel) and "vinhático" (Madeira mahogany)). It extends over 15 thousand hectares, around 20% of Madeira's surface, covered by the Parque Natural da Madeira in a band between 600 and 1300 metres above sea level which is very humid and has frequent fog. Despite its size the truth is that most of the places where the forest is best preserved are not easy to access. Good options are the Levada do Caldeirão Verde which begins in Queimadas in Santana or the Rabaçal "levadas" which are on the north of the island. In the Laurissilva forest there are also bushes and herbaceous plants which stand out on account of the beauty of their flowers such as leituga, broom, Helichrysum melaleucum, Bowles wallflowers, geraniums, Persian buttercups and Pride of Madeira. Birdwatchers will not be disappointed – it is possible to spot firecrests, blackbirds and long-toed pigeons as well as predatory birds such as buzzards and kestrels.

Pride of Madeira and an endemic Madeiran lizard.

*Examples of the **Dragon Tree** at Sítio das Neves, São Gonçalo, Funchal*

The Dragon Tree

In the past these trees were common on the south coast of Madeira and Porto Santo. A precious red dye known as dragon's blood used to be extracted from them. It is possible that this was the purpose of the first incursions into Madeira. Today they only exist in gardens more or less throughout Funchal.

Across the peaks

Vereda do Homem em Pé *between Pico Ruivo and Achada do Teixeira*

IN THE south-facing mountains that rise to greater altitudes vegetation is scarce and the landscape is steep with spectacular views. A good choice is the seven kilometre path between Pico do Areeiro to Pico Ruivo which connects the two highest points on the island and takes about three hours. The path takes you over peaks, round enormous mountains surrounded by deep valleys in which silence reigns. Close to the beginning of the path is the nesting place of the Zino's petrel, a bird in danger of extinction. It was here, in the centre of the island, that the biggest volcanic eruptions occurred. The terrain is very eroded and in several places it is possible to see the basalt network, the result of lava infiltration between softer volcanic materials. It resembles a checkered structure holding up the great peaks – in places where soft materials predominated, erosion by rain and flowing water was implacable, taking everything with it and carving out valleys whose walls are sometimes sheer. For most of the walk vegetation is sparse.

Climbing up to Pico Ruivo things change and the path crosses a wood of tree heaths. Having arrived at the shelter it is another half an hour to the top of Pico Ruivo where it is possible to enjoy the spectacle of the clouds racing up the northern slopes and pouring down into the Curral das Freiras valley. From here there are two options: turning back or dropping down to Achada do Teixeira, another very beautiful walk which has the advantage of being much easier; in this case it is best to organise to be collected beforehand.

Cuisine

One of Madeira's specialities is the so-called "peixe fino", locally caught fish which is often seen in the Funchal market and in some restaurants. Black "espada" (scabbard fish) is another classic in Funchal where it has been a staple since its discovery in the XIXth century. It can be prepared in several ways: fillets, fried in steaks (known locally as "rolos") or "em caldeira" (a kind of single fish hotpot cooked in a light tomato and onion stock). Tuna, nowadays fished in the Azores by the fishermen from Caniçal, is prepared "escabeche" style by marinating and frying, in steaks or salted for one day and then cooked. When it comes to meat, pork is cut into cubes after having been marinated in "vinha d'alhos" (vinegar and garlic), a traditional Christmas dish. Beef "espetadas" (skewers) originated at the "arraiais" (street festivals) where they are consumed in great quantity accompanied by "bolo do caco", a bread cooked on a heated stone. "Milho frito" (fried cubes of cold polenta) is an increasingly popular accompaniment. Some restaurants are also reviving old country recipes such as "sopa de carne" (meat soup) and "sopa de trigo" (wheat soup) and "caldos da romaria" (meat and vegetable broth).

"Bolo do caco"

Birdwatching

BIRDWATCHERS have much to observe in Madeira including several endemic birds. There are two alternatives: to walk from Pico do Areeiro to Achada do Teixeira where it is possible to spot the Eurasion Sparrow-hawk, Berthelot's pipit, Plain swift, long-toed pigeon, red-breasted robin, chaffinch, rock sparrow, Zino's petrel (a bird saved from extinction by a Madeiran ornithologist, Paul Alexander Zino) and the firecrest; or a walk as short and easy (half an hour) as it is beautiful, the Vereda dos Balcões from Ribeiro Frio which crosses a patch of Laurissilva in which it is possible to observe all the birds which live in this forest.

The "Festa"

Madeira's big festival is traditionally known simply as the "Festa". It takes place between Christmas Eve, or the evening before, and carries on until New Year's Day. The 23rd is the last shopping day. Many people do not work from the 24th to the 27th. After Christmas Eve and midnight mass there is a night of partying followed by Christmas day dedicated to the immediate family during which it is taboo to go outside the home. Contrary to that which happens in other countries and mainland Portugal, the main festive meal is Christmas lunch when traditionally "carne de vinha d'alhos" (pork marinated in vinegar and garlic) and "bolo de mel" (honey cake) are eaten. The 26th and 27th are known as the "primeira oitava" and "segunda oitava" and are dedicated to visiting the extended family and friends. New Year's Eve is a big tourist event (featured in the Guinness Book of Records as from 2006 for having the world's biggest firework display). But for Madeirans it is much more than that. Especially in Funchal where seeing in the new year watching the fireworks with the family is a must, a ritual almost as important as Christmas. Afterwards it is customary to go out all, or almost all, night.

The summer "arraiais"

DURING the summer there are "arraiais" (street festivals) almost every weekend wherever there is a church or chapel. These are religious festivals with processions on ephemeral carpets of flowers. The irreverent side of the festival basically consists of eating large quantities of meat accompanied by "bolo do caco" (bread) and wine, all sold from wooden stalls. Another attraction are the amateur music groups playing and singing on request where it is still possible to see traditional instruments such as the "rajão" (a kind of ukelele), "viola de arame" (a nine-stringed guitar) or the "braguinha" (a small four-stringed guitar).

View from the Vila Guida viewpoint, Estrada Conde de Carvalhal

The city of Funchal

Santa Maria

Considered one of the oldest in Funchal, Rua de Santa Maria is the main street in this part of the city. It has always retained its popular spirit with a population traditionally dedicated to fishing and other crafts. With its low, green-shuttered houses – a leitmotif of Madeiran architecture – and cobble streets, Rua de Santa Maria is one of the most attractive streets in city. It begins in Largo do Poço next to the place where Santa Maria Maior Church once stood, the church having been destroyed by the 1803 floods, and ends in Largo do Socorro. In front of the church there is a viewpoint

with a beautiful view over the city. On the way you can take a detour to look at the Corpo Santo Chapel. Continuing along Rua do Portão to the right of the chapel you may visit the São Tiago Fortress constructed in the XVIIth century which today houses the Museum of Contemporary Art that has an interesting collection of contemporary Portuguese art. If you take the alley to the right before reaching the fortress you will reach the beach where you can see rowing boats, the last vestiges of the fishing industry in the quarter. For many decades Marítimo, Madeira's most popular football club, played where today there is the Almirante de Reis Public Garden and the cable car's seafront terminal.

Corpo Santo Chapel. *Originally built in the XVth century it was connected to an order which functioned as a social welfare association for the fishermen*

The Sé parish

What is considered to be
the second oldest quarter in
Funchal is located between
Ribeira de João Gomes and
the Sé Cathedral; this is
where the sugar merchants
settled in the XVth century.
It is an area with traditional
shops, almost uninhabited
but buzzing with life during
the day. Coming from the
Sé you will see Largo do
Pelourinho and the imposing
building of the old Companhia
Insular de Moinhos factory.
Crossing the bridge over
Ribeira de Santa Luzia you
will find the beginning of
Rua da Alfandega, the
backbone of the quarter,
with its rows of popular
shops almost all housed in
XVIIIth buildings. Other
shopping streets branch off
this one – Rua dos Tanoeiros
(cask manufacturers), Rua do
Esmeraldo (where the house
of this Flemish merchant who
hosted Christopher Columbus
used to be) and Rua do Sabão.
The road ends very close to
the Sé which was built on
the orders of Manuel I.

São Pedro

The parish of São Pedro still
has an aristocratic atmosphere.
Special mention goes to Rua
da Carreira with its palatial
houses from the XVIIth, XVIIIth
and XIXth centuries where
Isabella de França stayed.
Walking up Rua do Surdo you
will reach Largo de São Pedro
where you will find the old
family residence of the Count
of Carvalhal, today the
Municipal Library and Museum.
Next door you should not miss
the Dr. Frederico de Freitas

Funchal Cathedral, Rua da Carreira

House-Museum which used
to belong to the book collector
who discovered Isabella de
França's manuscript. In the
surrounding area, a visit to
the Madeira Wine Company's
São Francisco Wine Lodges
in Avenida Arriaga is a must,
as well as to the Museum
of Saced Art in Rua do Bispo
and the Colégio Church,
a Jesuit place of worship
dating from the XVIIth
century and now restored.

Contemporary architecture

HERE are some suggestions for those who like to view modern and contemporary architecture. The renowned Mercado dos Lavradores is a beautiful building which is representative of Portuguese modernism from the 1940's (Edmundo Tavares). An important Portuguese architect from a later generation, Raul Chorão Ramalho, has many works in Madeira of which one perhaps stands out: the Regional Parliament building on Avenida do Mar. The Casino Park Hotel was designed by one of the most famous XXth century architects, Oscar Niemeyer. More recent architectural works include Gonçalo Byrne's intervention in

Casa das Mudas Arts Centre by Paulo David
*The **Casino Park Hotel**, the only example of Niemeyer's work in Portugal*

the Clube Naval. Younger architects have also been at work on Madeira: Tiago Oliveira in the Estalagem da Ponta do Sol and, in particular, a rising star, Paulo

David (ICA Award 2006), with special mention going to the Centro das Artes / Casa das Mudas in Calheta which was nominated for the Mies Van der Rohe prize in 2005.

Madeira Story Centre

Come and see and feel Madeira's history in three dimensions. Observe the first volcanic eruptions, old maps in their original sizes, see how the personalities in this book looked and dressed, how the sugar mill worked, savour the smell of the wine and spices – and at the end you can sit down on board an Aquila seaplane from which you can see the view as it was at the time.

The museum

The Madeira Story Centre, which opened in 2005, is based on an innovative concept – an interactive museum – which uses sounds and smells to recreate the atmosphere of times gone by. The history of Madeira is presented chronologically by means of reproductions of objects from different periods, mannequins which represent historical figures, small scale models and games. From the volcanoes to the seaplanes, not forgetting the wise men of Greece, pirates, navigators and other celebrities, the key facts are displayed in an entertaining and uncomplicated approach.

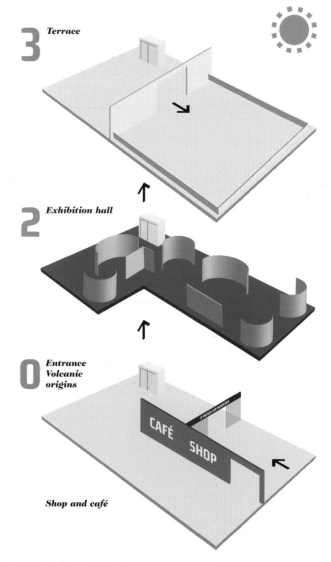

3 Terrace

2 Exhibition hall

0 Entrance
Volcanic
origins

CAFÉ SHOP

Shop and café

Madeira Story Centre

The shop

On the ground floor there is a shop where you will find a variety of carefully selected items for sale – from regional specialities like "bolo de mel" (honey cake), fennel and Madeira wine sweets to books specialised in nature tourism, travel guides and maps as well as puppets, learning games and note books. A unique shop in Madeira.

The Café

There is also a café in the foyer of the museum. Here you can savour the best of Madeira's sweets while reading books on the history of the island in the small library.

The Terrace

On the roof of the museum there is a terrace with a panoramic view over the sea and various plants endemic to the island which are part of the permanent exhibition. Events such as receptions, cocktail parties and special dinners can also be hosted here with the catering provided by the client or the museum.

Madeira Story Centre

HISTORY AND CULTURE

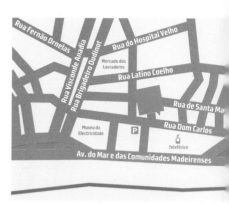

Rua D. Carlos I, 27-29
9060-051 Funchal – Madeira
Located right in front of the city
cable car
Telephone: (+351) 291 000 770
Fax: (+351) 291 000 789
Site: www.storycentre.com
info@storycentre.com

Opening times
Museum: 10.00 – 18.00
Shop: 10.00 – 19.00
Open every day of the week
Closed on 25th December

Mrs Jean Cockerell
Memories of Madeira
Patchwork donated by the artist
after her visit to the Madeira
Story Centre in September 2005